Perfect Poetry

or 'Worthless Words'

by Paul Taylor

Foreword by the Author

This collection is dedicated to my late wife, Kay, who was taken too soon by brain cancer in 2020. She was the most wonderful person and I miss her terribly. Kay was intelligent, witty, loving, generous and, as you can see, beautiful. She was also most discerning – she wasn't keen on my poetry!

Nevertheless, I hope you find something to engage you in this collection of snippets from my life. Should there be any financial proceeds from these efforts, they will all go to The Brain Tumour Society. Please scan the QR code should you wish to donate. Thank you so much for your support,

Paul Taylor.

Donate to The Brain
Tumour Charity

Contents

Section 2   39

Section 3   66

Section 1

My Photograph Album

If it don't make you laugh
If it don't make you cry
If it don't make you angry
Or wonder why
If it don't inspire
Or don't engage
Just worthless words
On a pointless page.

Virgin

I confess I'm a Virgin

With this poetry stuff.

So please when you take me...

Don't abuse me...

– Too much

Do treat me gently,

Don't judge me...

– Too soon

So, I might, in due course

Come to mean more...

– To You

A Picture of You

Silken scrolls gently unfold,
A tide of tender embrace.
Cradling in such delicate hold,
Your soft accepting face.
Then nonchalant, flowing easily on
In a magical dance of grace.

Sunlight begging permission,
Dapples kisses on your skin.
Warm rays that glisten and ripple,
As if with the coming of Spring.
Would that I occupy such favoured position,
Then never could night slide in.

My gaze enraptured by amber brown,
Fixated by knowing eyes.
Benevolent beacons shining, profound,
So loving, so tender, so wise.
A place in which I would surely drown,

My picture of paradise.

Country Flies

Swirling, swerving, here and there,
Three, four, forty – swarming everywhere.
Thorax-clad with Teflon sheen
Of rainbow hues from red to green,
Drive those whirring buzzing machines.

Bulbous eyes reflect the glare,
Beneath pointed heads devoid of hair,
But aero-dynamic, built for speed.
What an accomplished flying machine!

But short on beauty, shorter on style,
Been behind these bums for half a mile!

Not There

Alone don't mean lonely,
Wary don't mean scared.
No shove don't mean no purpose,
Defer don't mean don't dare.
Frailty don't mean weakness,
Watching on don't mean don't care.
Silence don't mean nothing to say,
No show don't mean no flair.
No sigh don't mean there's no relief,
Nor hurt – there is repair.
No god don't mean there's no belief,
Unseen don't mean not there.

Casanova Ventosa

Sotto voce – the purr of the hoover,
A seductive sensual sound.
No courtships could ever be smoother,
Gliding graciously over the ground.

Stoccato pecks on the staircase,
The landing is next to succumb,
To the charms of the silky romancer,
And his irresistible hum.

Caramente caressing the carpets,
Flirting fondly with the floors,
A dance of romance in the bedroom,
Then a racy romp in the hall.

La cucina, the lounge and the diner,
La *ventosa* seduces each scene,
Casanova, the *aspiapolvere,*
And consummate love machine.

The Show

The lights are dimmed, the crowd muddles in
Then settles down for the show.
They're here to watch the children dance,
As the anticipation grows.
The dancers wait aside the stage,
With nerves to overcome.
Getting changed to entertain,
Their siblings, dads and mums.

Gathered in soldierly order,
Waiting in the wings,
The clock counts down, the lights go up,
And the pulsating music begins.

Prancing out to the piper's tune
The children enact their routine.
This, the first of several tonight
With costume changes between.

A different dance, befitting of age,
Each performance, a bouquet of cheer.
Seasoned teens, to tots, so keen,
(Though some are frozen with fear!)

The show rolls along, song after song,
With such energy, timing and grace.
Fluid transitions, pointed precision,
And professional smiles on their face.

Like birds on the wing, drawing one in
To a frieze of poetical poise.
A tapestry to the beauty of youth -
Their expression of innocent joy.

The finale comes and the evening is done,
Closed with flowers and praise.
Rapturous applause then the opening of doors
As the dancers troop from the stage.

Now silent and bare, as if nothing there,
Save shadows from safety lights ....
But not everything's gone, for the presence lives on
Of the dancers who stole the night.

Internet Stalkers

I never invited invasion like this,
Wanton intrusion I cannot resist.
A tsunami of adverts
A barrage of 'noise',
Indigestible cookies,
The marketing ploy.

Pay the ransom or bear the abuse,
Of the profiteering that aims to seduce
And then to impose itself on me,
Without a care for my privacy.

And why should I pay to be left alone,
Protection money, just like Capone?
Even then, there's no guarantee,
They won't be coming back for me.

Consider Alexa – that 'cute' little thing,
Surreptitiously listening in
Its masters compute then duly decree
Exactly what it is that I need.

Those algorithms that analyse,
Record, compile and synthesise
To generate the hologram,
Of what I should be – not who I am.

Who can oppose abusers like these?
The Mothers of digital tyranny
Just let me do and let me be.
Stalk somewhere else – and stop stalking me.

SnuffleTruffle & Spikey

SnuffleTruffle Hedgepig,
To give you her full name.
Is a dainty little hedgehog,
Who loves playing tickly games.

She has a friend called 'Spikey,'
Who looks so fierce-some,
Because he has such prickly spikes
From his ears down to his bum.

One night, whilst out foraging
With her nose stuck to the ground,
SnuffleTruffle shuffled round
And guess what Snuffle found?

Underneath a pile of leaves,
Lay Snuffle's favourite treat.
SnuffleTruffle had found a truffle,
A thing she loved to eat.

Meanwhile, Spikey, hungry too
Found a bowl of cream.
On the doorstep of a gentle man
All for him, it seemed.

"That man put out a tasty dish,
Just for me to find."
Spikey lapped it up and wished,
More folks would be so kind.

Trouble was, that milky meal
Was not for him, in fact,
Greedy Spike had eaten the tea
Of the next-door neighbour's cat!

Just then, the neighbour's cat appeared,
And she was not best pleased,
When she saw that hedgehog Spikey
Had gobbled up her tea.

She hissed at him, arched her back,
And opened up her claws.
Spikey thought, "She's going to attack,"
And rolled into a ball.

The cat jumped up and landed
On Spikey's prickly coat.
His spikes stuck up and pierced her skin,
With lots of little holes.

Puss wailed in pain, jumped off again,
She scarpered double quick.
Spikey thought, "It's alright now,"
Then started to be sick.

"Oh, I feel so ill," groaned Spikey,
Slowly turning green.
"I must my find my good friend Snuffle,
She'll know what's wrong with me."

So off he crawled into the woods,
And sniffed SnuffleTruffle out.
Though hedgehogs cannot see too well,
They have such smelly snouts.

When he finally found her
He confided to his friend,
While milky stuff came from his mouth,
And from the other end!

SnuffleTruffle was horrified,
At Spikey, drinking cream.
"You must never touch such milky things,
Yummy though they seem".

"For if you are a hedgehog,
Too much of it can kill,
You're lucky it was just one bowl,
But no wonder that you're ill."

"Stick to what you're meant to eat,
Kitten food and slugs
And truffles if you find them...
Oh, Spikey, come and look..."

And there upon the forest floor
Lay her special treat.
SnuffleTruffles' snuffled truffle
For both of them to eat.

They sat down on the leafy ground,
And enjoyed their hearty feast.
Then both felt rather drowsy
And gently fell asleep.

They lay there, oh so peacefully,
So cosy and so snug
And dreamed of lots of lovely things,
Like snuffling worms and bugs.

SnuffleTruffle woke up first,
And saw Spikey in a doze.
Quietly, she crept up on him,
And tickled his little toes.

Spikey woke up straightaway,
And let out a mighty shriek.
But Snuffle kept on tickling him,
Until he couldn't speak.

How they laughed, they had such fun
Now Spikey was alright.
But never ever put out milk
For hedgehogs, day or night!

Lido Deck - 16

The Lavinia – such a lovely ship,
But there's something quite obscene.
Wallowing on an upper deck,
On Lido Deck – 16.

Where burgers face their genocide,
And chips and pizzas scream.
A cornucopia of calories,
On Lido Deck – 16.

The frenzied gorging orgies,
Of pure lascivious greed.
Bloated porcines bloating more,
On Lido Deck – 16.

Sunbeds' backs are breaking,
Though their tortured groans suppressed
'Neath the bulging of the gluttonous,
On Lavinia's 16th deck.

At sea with mass obesity,
A glump of gelatine.
A coagulation of cholesterol
On Lipo Deck – 16.

Confinement

How come I snatch the mobile
when I hear it ring?
How come I curse those others,
who want to tell me things?
How come I count those wasted days
until we next will meet?
How come time's suspended
when at last, we get to speak?
How come I choose to share with you,
what no other could guess?
How come my tablet's lost its charge
and my phone won't take your texts?
How come you're taking holiday,
then struck by malady?
How come you have so much to do,
that excludes my company?
How come you re-ignite my life,
after all that I've been through?
How come I'm to myself confined,
while I crave confined with you?

A Visit to the Dentist

Prelude

Though I clean my teeth religiously,
Today it's done fastidiously.
Brush them up and brush them down
Under the gums and all around.
Got to make them look their best
For today is their six monthly check.

Out of date Magazines

I approach the girl behind the desk
Busied with purpose and primly dressed,
But with welcoming smile and gracious, "Hello",
I trade in light banter so my nerves won't show.

Of course, she has seen this all before
But she feigns that she hasn't, and points to the door
Through which I must pass, to an assortment of chairs
And pretend not to notice the other folks there.

The minutes drag on, folks come, and then go.
When is it my turn, I don't want to know?
My tension - come terror, mustn't be seen,
So I bury myself in an old magazine.

One which I so randomly chose,
From the dishevelled pile of whatever, who knows?
A Woman, a Home, a Vanity Fair,
My mind nebulised, I pretend I'm not there.

Then reality strikes as I am found,
By a silhouetted woman in clinical gown.
Quizzically, invitingly, but with sinister tone,
She beckons me follow, to a fate unknown.

The Reckoning (1)

"Hello Mr Fortune, how are you today?"
"I'm fine," I lied, not wanting to say.
Instead, a reprise of temerity,
Rejoined with polite sincerity.

"Please come over, sit in the chair,
You can put your jacket over there.
Now I'm going to tip you back,
Put on these glasses and try to relax."

My would-be tormentor took her place to my right
To my left her assistant, both suspiciously nice.
Then a suite of bright lights was shone in my face
And so they began to consider my case.

She leaned over me gently, I looked into her eyes.
Benevolent, beautiful, my trust reconciled,
With my imagined tormentor, and her partner in pain.
I looked at her in wonder, but then looked away.

"Open wide, a little wider please"
And the litany of defeats proceeds.
Occlusal, distal, mesial, the lot,
Tombstones attesting to battles well lost.

The sojourn is over, I'm lifted back up
And invited to rinse from the plastic cup.
I remove the goggles and sip tentatively,
And spit into the bowl so delicately.

Careful not to make a mess,
unbecoming from dignified guests.
I picked up my jacket, straightened the sleeves,
And moved to the door, reluctant to leave.

The Reckoning (2)

But withdraw I must and with a touch of regret,
I descend the stairs to the girl at the desk,
Who politely informs me how much I must pay
For the privilege of my turbulent day.

The card machine chatters its evident glee.
No need for injections, or empathy.
It performs the extraction with clinical skill
And leaves a hole so hard to fill.

Nanny In Her Alley

The grandkids come round at least three times a week
To see their Nanny work her street.
In total command of her culinary stage
As she roves up and down
So that meals can be made.
Eggs in the morning and pizzas for tea,
All for the grand-kids, leftovers for me.

Imperiously striding along in her aisle,
A magnificent woman who does it with style.
But it's not just the cooking – there's a secret to tell,
When the kids have gone home
She does dancing as well.
Forget Pan's People, she knows how to move,
My private dancer in her kitchen groove.

Her shape is delighting, her movement exciting.
Sometimes quite frightening, but always enticing.

Morning comes round,
They're not here again!
"Oh yes Grampy, and here tomorrow"
"And the day after to add to your sorrow."

Nanny is back patrolling her galley
(Although tonight, she'll encore at the Palais).
For now, the day gig but still the same sight
Of a beautiful Nanny serving delight.

Grampy In Nanny's Alley!

Nanny's away – each dog has its day
Now Grampy's in charge of breakfast – hooray!
Sprouts and cabbage but not much for tea
And a slice of dry bread to accompany
The gourmand delights of Grampy's cuisine
And cordon bleu that's rarely been seen.

"You can't cook Grampy, I'll show you how."
"Three eggs in the bowl then whisk them up now."
"Thank you Ella but I'm in control,"
"Into the micro-wave out of the bowl."
"You're wrong again Grampy, it goes in the pan,"
"Please come back our wonderful Nan."

The grandkids come round at least three times a week
But when Grampy's cooking they seek a retreat.
So as to get some half-decent grub,
They insist that we all, go down to the pub.

Good At Something

Ella aged 8

"Grampy, you're just being annoying".
"Well, I'm glad that I'm good at something."
"Grampy, it's not a compliment!"
"You're the most annoying thing ever!"
"The most annoying thing in the whole entire house!"

Stomp stomp stomp stop.
(Mummy is in the hall)
"Hi kids, what's the noise all about?"
"Mummy, Grampy is <u>so</u> annoying
– he's the cause of it all!"

Poop-Scooping

"There's a pooh on the patio" she stoutly declares.
"I don't think it's mine love – I think that it's theirs."
By "theirs" I mean the resident dogs
Who don't have recourse to the indoor bogs.
But were they inside, I'd take care to say "sit"
(For fear of mispronouncing it!)

A Round Tuit

(Dedicated to Mira)

"I nearly got round to it"
(*The hoovering, that is*)
"I was about to do it"
(*Sort out the fridge*)
"Just give me a moment"
(*Help find the spoons*)
"I'll be with you shortly"
(*Where are you?*)"
"Something cropped up"
(*Have you done it yet?*)
"I'll make a note"
(*Can you phone the vet?*)
"I must show you how "
(*Put the heating on?*)
"It's much too dark"
(*Walked the dogs?*)
"I'll do it tomorrow"
(*Can you call 999?*)
"Is it important?"
(*I think that I've died!*)

Section 2

Money, Money, Money.

"Surely, you've heard of Guinea pigs,
Perhaps you have one at home.
But do you know what a Guinea is ....
It's twenty-one shillings, you know."

"Don't be so silly, who's heard of a shilling?"
"Well, it's twelve old pennies you see".
*"But how can Penny be part of a Guinea,
She's a girl who's stood next to me."*

*"Guineas are made of noses and teeth,
Legs and feet and eyes,
Whiskers and fur and fat fluffy tummies,
But there can't be a Penny inside?"*

"No, you've misunderstood, it's not Penny the girl,
Though that'd be rather funny.
I'm not playing games but a Guinea's the same,
They're both a kind of money."

"Then, the number of pennies that add up to a pound,
Is two hundred and forty for sure.
So, look after your pennies to take care of your pounds,
And then you can buy much more."

"So much for pennies, what about shillings,
Don't they count at all?"
"Yes, the number of shillings that make up a pound,
Is twenty, it's called a score."

"What, like the result of a football game
Where teams can draw two all?"
"No, in counting, a score is twenty,
No less and nothing more."

"The football team that's top of the league,
Wins the champion's crown.
Now a crown is a hat, but it's more than that,
Five shillings is what you lay down."

"But if you can't afford this amount,
Try for a half instead."
"No-one would frown at half a crown,
It's better than staying in bed!"

"Now half a crown is thirty pennies,
And should you not have enough,
A florin is twenty-four of them,
Which is fine if times are rough."

"A florin is a shilling times-ed by two,
And a shilling in pennies, is twelve.
I say this again just to remind you,
In case you'd forgotten by now!"

"A shilling is also two sixpences,
Which in Christmas puddings reside.
A shilling is also four thruppenny bits,
Which are yellow and have eight sides."

"Two ha'pennies make up a penny,
And four farthings do so too.
And after that, there isn't any ....
Any more money for you!"

pOOp Deck - 18

bOOb Deck - 18

A testimony
To a victory
Of gravity.

One shouldn't know,
But if old girls show
Their droopy boobs so avidly,
One can't help but note -
(With averting eyes),
The flaccid sacks that once had size –
Firmness and good shape maybe?
What do they think us men do see?

"No, I want an even tan,
To show my blooms to any man,
Whose gaze I'll capture – make him keen".
Ladies – some things are best left –

- Unseen.

Devil Dog Spike

Devil Dog Spike our black spaniel relation
Came to our house for his summer vacation.
He's been here three weeks now, may God damn & blast him.
Our nerves and our furniture may not outlast him!

Devil Dog Spike has a mind of his own.
He turns our chickens to feather and bone.
Our bedroom curtains, our carpets, our sofa,
There isn't anything he won't pee over!

The donkey's gone mental, the ducks lost their 'quack'.
Our cats they went AWOL and never came back.
The geese all stopped laying, while our dogs just cower.
As Devil Dog Spike up-roots all our flowers!

The old horse has bolted and thrown off a shoe.
But Spike is elated at eating the horse pooh.
Devil Dog Spike I have only one wish
Be-devil our livestock but please spare the fish!

Devil Dog Spike our black spaniel relation
Wreaked on our homestead complete devastation.
Spike has gone home now, and so we thank God.
For one year's deliverance from that Devil Dog!

Victim

So you're a victim
Who can't make the change,
To the life you are living,
So, a victim remain.
Holding the ground
Which none can invade,
You're safe as a victim,
Who can't make the grade.
Dragging down those
Who endure the shame,
Of thinking it's their fault,
Pawns in your game
Of being the victim
They are to blame.
Not you in your misery
Your hopeless state
It's everything out there
That's determined your fate.
Nothing at all to do with you.
"It's so unfair, what else can't you do?"

A Pleasant Summer's Evening

Wood pigeons wooing,
Displaying and cooing,
Blackbirds trilling their thrill.
Robins bobbing,
Jackdaws gobbing,
But then the evening went Stihl.

No Flies on Me

Contact-less, so mostly blind,
Bothered by some pesky flies.
Grope for 'Raid' and hit the spray,
Make those little blighters pay!

Flies still there but a musky scent,
Not 'Raid' but anti-perspirant.
And from this tale, it's plain to see,
Just why there are no flies on me!

The Sock

Wash day for those unsanitary clothes,
It's that time of the week.
As the bedroom casket overflows,
With its prisoners begging release.

Casting them down to the floor below,
If rags had bones they'd break.
Nevertheless, their flailings foretell,
Of a hell beyond escape.

Gather the victims up from the ground,
Ready to face the machine,
Which, in its swirling dervish delight,
Will drown, boil, and fling them about around,
Yet no-one none will heed their screams.

But wait, what's that, lying still, on the tiles
Languishing in its plot?
To evade the fate of the rest of the pile,
A single solitary sock!

And so, bending down, and fumbling round,
Enduring the pain in my back,
The recalcitrant item is duly retrieved,
And returned to the rest of the pack.

Crossing to the utility room,
Determined to stick to my theme,
Stuff the drum with the wretched scum
And powder to render it clean.
The time has come, press 'start' to run
The drown and boil routine.

The cycle complete, drag out the debris
Transfer the pile to the dryer,
Then bake the cakes at one-eighty degrees
In this, their funeral pyre.

[But wait, what's that, lying still, on the tiles,
Languishing in its plot?
To avoid the fate of the rest of the pile
That single, solitary sock].

Ever defiant, it had ducked the appliance,
Smug at not having been cooked.
I'll hang it outside
To dangle and dry
Until it's finally kaput.

Don't make the mistake of trying to escape!
(As it's you I have my eye on)
From the steaming, scalding, screaming, and folding.
"Hey, but aren't socks exempt from the iron?"

Pleat the defeated along their creases
And bear them upstairs for the drawers.
Matching the pairs, something's not there,
Perhaps it fell to the floor?

Ah yes, what's that, lying still, on the mat?
Still languishing in its plot
To evade the fate of the rest of the pack
That feckless, frigin' sock.

Morphine Dreams

A patient in an opposite bed
Lying next to a Shiatzu.
Hairy spiders crawl up the wall,
I can see them – can you?

Outside a lean-to toilet
In a shuttered garden I like,
After saying goodbye to my daughter
And her beautiful mother, my wife.

A farmhouse with a huge mirror
I see through - To a pond.
People, dogs, and a flock of sheep
Who toward me cautiously creep,
I move, they freeze, then abscond.

Then I'm taken - to be repaired – downstairs,
A vasectomy – to make me safe
By an efficient nurse, while I'm awake.

In séance with others, they moan as a team,
Humming their sense of tranquillity.
A junior is a substitute
On one of the spinning machines.

He does really fine
Given it's his first time.
But my leg is restrained by his weave,
So I try to shake it – to shake it free.

Now I'm in a beauty salon
Can I be returned to the ward soon, please?
"My wife went on a fishing trip
this weekend", says the nurse.
I ask him how it went
– the response? "It could have been worse."

There's a Harry Shaw coach waiting outside,
To take the séance folks back.
Now I can prove what has happened to me
By reading the Telegraph ads.

I came to in a B & Q store
With a nurse who understood
To combine recovery with D.I.Y., -
that really must be good.

People scream - in terrible pain,
Just down from the bed
In an unseen room.
Physio in a drowning pool?
I beg the nurse for a peeing pot,

But she is wont to refuse
And queries why I need it
Cue severe abuse.

I'm in a deep and darkened state,
But I've been here already
So I comfort those lying with me.
"Don't worry, just stay steady."

There's an Irishman limping along with me,
By the boat where once confined
I hear a couple swimming,
Then swearing an oath of some kind.
Then the woman is there – my nurse with wet hair.

Is there something wrong with my mind?

The Re-Sit Result

I did go there, fully aware,
Intending that we would meet.
On the steps by the door
Where you sit your exam
- so uncomfortable, my retreat.
And then you emerge
With doubt in your face
And I question the teacher I am.

You sat down to join me
But with little belief.
I listened with sympathy,
Then offered you leave,
But you wouldn't go, to my relief.

You and I sat sitting, chatting alone,
Passing the time while you check your phone.
Then casually, you confide in me,
That I'm the best ever teacher you've known.

There we still were
My reserve overthrown,
But with privilege and pride
At my place in your life
So good to be sat on that stair.

The news comes through...

Both ecstatic, elated, the steps are vacated,
By a very proud teacher
and a much relieved you.

Autumn

Slowly, gently, swirling round,
Autumn leaves fall to the ground.
No life left, no wings to fly,
Autumn comes - and so to die,
Those leaves, once green - now brittle brown,
Softly, sadly, tumble down.

Yet await the Spring and then we'll see,
The blooming of another tree
Whose wakened fruits caress a sun,
That shines a-bright of life begun,
From the denouement that went before
Yet I can see only Winter – nothing more.

Giggly and Cute
(Dedicated to Yvette)

I have a good friend, she's giggly and cute,
Especially after a couple of flutes.
'Champers' is bubbly - she is so too!
She's also as lovely - a premier cru!

Baron von Bluebottle

Baron von Bluebottle was a great big fly.
So big in fact, he ruled the sky.
He buzzed and whirled round and round.
Never stopping to touch the ground.

Always mean and never nice
He loved to bully little flies.
He'd chase them so ferociously,
They'd tumble down so wearily.

This awful scene went on some time,
With little flies so often crying
"Will this torture never end,"
Could Bluebottle ever be their friend?

Then one day, under a bright blue sky
There appeared a beautiful dragonfly.
Sun beams danced upon her wings,
She really was the prettiest thing.

She saw the flies, so scared and sad,
And gently asked, "Are things so bad"?
The flies explained the goings on
Dragonfly said, "Well that's so wrong."

"Let me see what I can do,
To get you out of this terrible stew".
"What's taking place is so unfair,"
And with that, Dragonfly took to the air.

Baron von Bluebottle was taken aback,
When dragonfly glided by so fast.
She stuck out her tongue and called him a twit!
Well, Bluebottle was having none of this!

He turned and charged as hard as he could,
But went hurtling past her, why? because ....
Dragonflies fly but also, they hover.
She'd stopped in mid-air, like she couldn't be bothered!

The Baron went on careering past,
And unable to stop, he suddenly crashed -
Straight into the trunk of a tree
And fell to the ground, unconsciously.

When he awoke, there were blurs all round,
But soon he could see all the flies in a crowd,
Gathered behind a most beautiful sight,
That lady dragonfly who had ended his flight.

She hovered toward him, a smile in her eyes,
And asked the Baron if he was alright.
"Yes, I'm ok, but I think I'm in love!"
"With the lady who tricked me high up above."

"So, marry me please, I'll always be nice.
I'll take care of you, and all the flies."

Now Dragonfly liked Bluebottle's bum,
And all in all, she thought him handsome,
And now he had promised to be a nice fly,
"Yes, I will marry you," she kindly replied.

Then they were married
What a wonderful end,
With the flies and the Baron
Now the bestest of friends!

Down Here

About those in wheelchairs
who somehow aren't there?

The person that's pushing,
the one with no choice,
Is the one who's addressed,
By that pitying voice.
Meanwhile, the victim,
condemned to the chair,
Sits knowing, un-noticed,
down here, not up there.
Where kindly people
approach and engage.
The dutiful keeper,
but not the encaged.

As a Bloke

As a bloke - it's alright to cry sometimes,
Especially when your old dog dies.

I can cope with it, as I have to deal with it,
But when I don't, I can't.

It's been a bad day coming
And a bad day going on.

The dog's with peace,
But I'm in pieces.

It's alright to cry sometimes – as a bloke.

Bang Bang Boom Boom ...

Bang Bang Boom Boom
Here's your next robotic tune
Wah Wah Whine Whine endure the keyboard screech
Female vocal, would-be global, next day obsolete.
No complication, duplication, rhythmic re-repeat
Can't be too crude but must allude
To sex to sell the beat.

Formulaic is how we play it
No need for too much else
For the mindless to be grooving it
Cogent dis-connect.

But I'm a prude and can't collude
With musak from the shelf
Unsophisticated, totally hate it
I just might kill myself.

And when I've died
Boom Boom Wah Whine,
Do not Abide with Me
Let me rest in peace, and grant release
From the hellish constancy of ...
...B-B-B-B...

Zoe's citation for her late son, David

See 'They Matter' poem on page 64

David Aitken died suddenly and unexpectedly of Type 1 Diabetes on 15th March 2022. David was three weeks short of his 20th birthday; a student living life to the full and loving it. He left heartbroken family and friends, including his twin sister, Sian. David's mother, Zoe, wrote this poem as she struggled with her loss.

Always in our hearts,
Always in our minds,
Always being missed.

They Matter

by Zoe Nichols

Our Children who no longer are,
They matter, they matter.
Tethered to a far-off star.
Always they will matter.

And down inside we feel them,
And wish they were still are.
And the tenses are confused
But grammar don't matter,

Because they are
Wherever we are.
As the moon goes down
And the sun comes up,
And every bad poetic trope,
They still bloody are.

And we remember the smiles,
And the first steps
Towards those stars,
Because they are
Where we are -
They so are.

A Reply

There once was a poet,
Who hid in a closet,
Pretending that she wasn't there,
But to pass the time,
She devoured the rhymes
Of those who posted her theirs.

Then she decided
To give up on hiding
And 'came out' from under the stairs.
She shared with another,
Who seemed like a brother,
Her beautiful words of despair.

The box had been opened,
Pandora had spoken,
And her words flew out over the sky.
Although they were little
They sparkled and glittered
Against the darkness of life.

Section 3

The Embrace

The surging swell of devotion
Demands of us both – release.
Insistent compulsion, impassioned conjunction;
The dams of reserve are breached.

Confluent currents drown each in the other
In a dizzying dance of desire.
Swirling, waltzing... the cadency falters,
And the magical maelstrom expires.

Breathless enrapture, so fleeting, so brief,
The insatiable torrents becalmed.
Discontentedly placid those waters so deep,
Back in their damned reservoirs.

Supermarket Trials

The odd and the hapless, the dazed and confused,
Directionless, dopy - the don't have a clue.
No orderly processions down these cluttered aisles,
They're all out here shopping
It may take a while.

Slew here and there, so not aware.
Dither and dally, obstruct every alley.
They make camp at the shelf, so I go somewhere else,
But they're still in the way,
I have a purpose - they have all day.

Now to the checkout ....
With vouchers that may, or may not be in date.
I'm next in the queue but I'll just have to wait.

"Have you our store card?" "Might have - not sure."
Seems like I'll just have to wait a bit more.
"Cash or card?"
"I do have the cash, wait while I ferret.
No I don't have enough, so I'll have to forget it."
"I do have a card though - it's in here somewhere,
Not sure where I left it, it's got to be there."
"Not to worry as I've found more cash.
Now I have to be going, as I do have to dash."

And doddle and dawdle towards the door.
You'll always get more - clogging the floor
"So sorry son."

My Mum Died Yesterday

My Mum died yesterday Yet we, her family, Perceive
"It's OK"?

- Somehow? She'd been so unable,

For such a long while Yet strived to be lucid - For us

To have a nice time -With Her And with her ready

- but difficult smile To confer. So, it's best it should end -
sooner

- than later? "It's what she'd have wanted,

- Wasn't it? "It's what WE would want,

After all, - Isn't it? And yet ... There is someone Who's
gone, Someone so dear, Who is never to be here - Again.

Never again

To give her a kiss That would be returned With so much
love So clumsily,

- And yet, So, forever, missed

I love you Mum, - X

Obstacles

Obstacles, obstacles everywhere...
Ruckled rugs on cluttered floors,
Shoes relax in frames of doors.
Doorsteps armed with lips to trip,
Obstacles everywhere.

Doors tightly sprung and closely hung,
A yard between no more
Push-pull, push-pull, push-pull before...

...Exhausted but at last the loo,
Though there's not now quite as much to do,
Save complete the job and then rehearse
Push-pull, push-pull, all in reverse.
Ordeal endured – despite the pain,
But it's been so long, I must go again!

Now a single disabled room
(with lip on floor and sprung front door).
A double bed and divan to boot,
Blocking almost every route.
Extra comfort – a low-slung chair,
Too low for me but I don't care
Because I can't get over there – anyway!

No walk-in shower but a generous bath.
Are hotel chains having a laugh?
Obstacles, obstacles everywhere.

A tourist town down by the sea,
Once again, I'd like a pee.
Conveniences inconvenient for me,
Because I need a radar key
400 yards up the hill.
Forgive me but I've lost the will.
Obstacles everywhere.

Lashes

The doors of the lift slide smoothly apart,
Inviting me in for the ride.
The menacing shadows evade my glance, as calmly, I step
inside.
But no buttons, no mirror, no room for manoeuvre,
Immersed in a jungle of ferns.
Young women confiding in sultry tones
Behind lashes, long and upturned.

Flickering, flapping, flirtatious fronds,
Allure then devour their prey.
Temptingly fanning and brushing my face,
As I feign to fight them away.
As the humid heat drains my resolve -
I resign myself to a tomb,
Encased in a Venus flytrap
And woven in fibrous cocoon.

Perfect Poetry

Properly prosecuted a perfect piece of poetry
but once begins a line of verse with a capital
yet only at its opening then ably aborts the curse
of all alliteration

and without exemption
full stops or any sign of punctuation   with
wholesome rhyme forbidden in full
yet closely contrived remarkably good

and with dissonant dis ...... location
a device to divide the flow --------
another sign of sophistication
all pointers to a
perfect piece of poetry.

Eulogy to My Father, John

He was always there for us,
Never one to moan.
He didn't ever want a fuss.
He didn't ever get one.

Silent strength his buttress
For us all to lean upon,
Though perhaps I only knew it
Once my Dad had gone?

Values not for compromise,
"Not right, then must be wrong."
Conversations minimised,
"Hallo?- I'll fetch your mom."

Except for working spaniels,
These, his greatest friends.
Then animated dialogue
And vast experience.

No trace, overt emotion,
Still rivers run so deep.
Yet immovable devotion
To Mom, also asleep.

Loving, sure and steadfast,
My memories of him.
I've lost a lifetime hero,
Now that Saint's gone marching in.

Daffalion and Dandydill

Daffalion and Dandydill
Were flowers in a border,
But their Gardener got their names confused
By saying them out of order.

Buttermum and Crysanthecup
Had suffered just the same,
But Primdrop and Snowrose
Rather liked their mixed up names.

Rosebell and Bluebush
Really didn't mind,
But by far the most unhappy
Were Celanweiss and Eideldine.

Both were rather snobbish,
In fact, you'd call them 'prudes'.
For if you get their names mixed up,
They think you're being rude!

The Grail

I can often remember how I felt,
Elation, confusion, rage,
But can rarely re-live the feeling itself,
If not caught, then confined to a page.

I posit the ink whose columns march East,
An emotionally charged crusade.
Staccato'd retreats, but then tireless reprise,
Until it has captured the Grail.

As the ink dries, and solidifies,
The prison is set and secure.
My feelings laid down, detained, crystallised,
There for the touching, of all.

While Time Permits

Forgive me but...

Please... may I steal a sip of a kiss,
A moment of daring, of magical bliss?

And please... may I take make a tenderful touch,
Only because I love you so much?

For the day will come when these treasures won't be
So meanwhile, pray, indulge me
In this...

Let me adore you, while time permits.

Clinging On

Don't denigrate the self-esteem,
What is left from where they've been.
The only constant left to them,
Clinging on to a long ago when
Things were good, less so now.
The way things were, much easier then.
Another day, and they're still here,
Another day to love, another day to fear.

A Prisoner of Hope

A prisoner of hope.
Yet hope is misguided disguise.
Reality Exists,
Not today but in a while
When the imposter reveals its real enterprise.
Then hope will extinguish along with my wife
And condemn me to exile
In a meaningless life.

My Anchor

The chain has been ripped and my anchor is gone.
Now, cut adrift, the restless sea grows
Increasingly strong.
Buffeted, battered, the boat pitches and rolls,
Though nothing now matters –
Out of control.
Tossing, yawing – an unforgiving tide,
The turmoil I feel in the deep, inside.

Wave Me Away

"Shall I go down to the sea today?"
So gently might it wash me away
From the wreckage dashed upon the shore,
And with wilful waves
Demand no more
Than for me to accept
Their soothing ebb,
But yet to neglect
Their return-ed dead.

A mothering sea
Embracing a son,
Holding him to her breast.
Firmly, but tenderly, bearing him on
To a place where he would rest.

That insistent unrelenting tide
Will forever ride and roll,
But without the debris
That once was me
No more that desperate soul.

Only Now

Only now can I begin to try
To remember the times with you ...

Months had dragged by, evading elapse
While I, locked-down, with my truth,
Succumbed to connive in a fatal collapse,
False comfort in self-abuse.

Spirits downed whole, to extinguish my soul,
My body consigned to die too.
No future, no present, nothing to hold,
What meaning had I, without you?

So I would not recall when I had it all
Yet now, there's a strange kind of peace.
My demons' devices now forestalled,
While soft ripples dance with my grief.

So as I begin to open my eyes
I rekindle lost belief
In reflections of our love and our life,
Though your being was all too brief.
Stolen from me, but you'll always be
The sweetest of my memories

My Kay, my heavenly wife.

Our Guardian

Who is with us
And everywhere besides.
Watch over what I and others do,
Always be our guide.
As I, and we, will get it wrong,
All too many times.

Forgive me for the pain I cause,
Help me show forgiveness too.
Let me learn self-sacrifice,
So to myself, I can be true.

Grant me the means to live a life,
Though chequered in what I do,
Where I may grow to realise
What you are
And Who
?

Wisdom

Some say that I'm wise and it's possibly true,
But any wisdom I have, I've had to accrue.
Unwanted intrusions disrupting the flow,
Of how and where my life should go.

Unsolicited gifts of unmerited grief,
Failure, regret, and betrayed belief.
Yet here am I, bruised and cut up,
But with the wisdom to know
I'm not wise enough.

Pathways

Pathways are long and pathways are short,
Rarely clear and so often fraught.
Strewn with thistles, thickets, and thorns,
Your body and soul so painfully torn.

Some lead to grief - despair untold
And convicted belief, it's the end of the road,
But no, there's still such a long way to go.
What awaits on your journey, no one can know.

But trust in yourself, you must go on,
For those who need you and bathe in your songs –
of joy, compassion, beauty, and care,
As we too have our paths, and our crosses to bear.

No matter the trials and torments to come,
With you our roads are festooned with love.
Loved by you, we don't travel alone ...

But neither is yours so lonely a road ...

For those whom you love, feel love for you too.
The light that you shine, reflected on you.
So permit yourself the warmth of the glow,
That is given to you, wherever you go.

She

She called me a Poet..., didn't she? - she did?
Could this really be true?
"No, I'm deluded, I must be so stupid,"
Those can't be the words she used.
Yet, I know they were said, was she leading me on?
Would anyone be so cruel?

Dare I be elated? Permit myself praise?
No, I can't indulge in pride.
I find these things too hard to accept,
Yet, I'm carried away by this tide,
Of learned opinion I have to respect,
Beside me, my literary guide.

Who knows where this might lead me,
Now I've bought the ticket to ride?
Might folks like my poetry?
I won't know until I've tried.
Meanwhile, I trust in my whirlwind,
She, who has blown my mind.

The End

Author's Acknowledgements

Many thanks to all who encouraged and cajoled me into compiling this book, friends, family and work colleagues. Special thanks to my longstanding friend Zoe, not only for her contribution 'They Matter', but also for her enthusiastic support. Many thanks to Mira for putting up with endless recitations of drafts of this work. I must mention my workmates Diana, Jackie and Yvette for their encouragement too; it was Yvette who, unbeknown to me, put me in touch with my would-be Editor, mentor and now good friend, Donna Edwards. Above is a poem (p88) I wrote immediately after our first meeting. Since then, Donna's guidance, "gentle edge" and patience have proved invaluable to me. Many thanks also to Stevie, Karen and Min, the other members of Rulers' Wit, publishers of this work.

Paul Taylor, September 2023.

Biography of the Author

Paul Taylor was born and raised a 'Shropshire Lad',
although he has spent the last 25 years in and around
Coventry. A college lecturer by day, as well as being a
qualified Chartered Accountant, Paul enjoys keeping and
training his Spaniels and aspires to be a bassist in a rock
band.

On occasions, he writes poems about things that move
him to do so. These had been filed away, until friends and
colleagues encouraged and then 'outed" him.
The result is this little book.

Printed in Great Britain
by Amazon

33093744R00056